WISDOM
from a
WOODSMAN

Ronnie Smith

WESTBOW
PRESS®
A DIVISION OF THOMAS NELSON
& ZONDERVAN

Copyright © 2017 Ronnie Smith.

All rights reserved. No part of this book may be used or reproduced by any means, graphic, electronic, or mechanical, including photocopying, recording, taping or by any information storage retrieval system without the written permission of the author except in the case of brief quotations embodied in critical articles and reviews.

Scripture quotations taken from the New American Standard Bible® (NASB), Copyright © 1960, 1962, 1963, 1968, 1971, 1972, 1973, 1975, 1977, 1995 by The Lockman Foundation Used by permission. www.Lockman.org

This book is a work of non-fiction. Unless otherwise noted, the author and the publisher make no explicit guarantees as to the accuracy of the information contained in this book and in some cases, names of people and places have been altered to protect their privacy.

WestBow Press books may be ordered through booksellers or by contacting:

WestBow Press
A Division of Thomas Nelson & Zondervan
1663 Liberty Drive
Bloomington, IN 47403
www.westbowpress.com
1 (866) 928-1240

Because of the dynamic nature of the Internet, any web addresses or links contained in this book may have changed since publication and may no longer be valid. The views expressed in this work are solely those of the author and do not necessarily reflect the views of the publisher, and the publisher hereby disclaims any responsibility for them.

Any people depicted in stock imagery provided by Thinkstock are models, and such images are being used for illustrative purposes only. Certain stock imagery © Thinkstock.

ISBN: 978-1-5127-9565-3 (sc)
ISBN: 978-1-5127-9564-6 (e)

Library of Congress Control Number: 2017911115

Print information available on the last page.

WestBow Press rev. date: 08/02/2017

To the memory of Barry K. Benton. His story of redemption has been used to change hundreds of lives. He was my friend. One day I will go where he is now.

I would like to thank my wife for her help with the editing process, her endless support of the work I do, and her tireless efforts at being a wife to me and a mom of five wonderful kids.

I would also like to thank the Lord for the experiences these stories have given me.

New books are seemingly being published at the speed of light these days. So this is just another book. My prayer is that it will encourage you to pursue Christ, to become like Him, and to let Him live through you. Some would ask, how can that be done through a book on hunting stories? Well, it's simple. I do not believe God wastes any experiences that we have. They're all for a purpose, and we can be pointed to the truth by all of them. So as you read the stories, experience the adventures, and then see the truth connection, you can begin to make the same connections with your own life stories.

Thanks for picking up a copy of this book. I pray it's a blessing to you. I sure had fun reliving these events as I wrote about them!

All game taken in this book was intended for the use of food.

—Ronnie Smith

Chapter 1

Getting Ready

When I go into the field to hunt an animal, be it a white-tailed deer, wild turkey, duck, goose, rabbit, or squirrel, I want to be equipped! I want to have the right weapon, ammo, calls, camouflage (camo), and a host of other things. The worst thing is to go into the field and realize too late that you're not prepared.

Let's take turkey hunting, for example. By the way, this is my favorite sport. Turkeys make my blood boil! (That is "hick" for saying they excite me, just in case you needed a translation. Most of those reading this book probably don't need a translation.)

When I go to the turkey woods, I want to be prepared. Here are some things I take with me: toilet paper, camo that matches the terrain I'll be hunting in, head net, gloves, hat, mouth calls, slate calls, box calls, crow calls, an owl call, gobble shaker, flashlight, decoys, Thermacell mosquito repellant and refills (especially if I'll be hunting in a swamp), a green rain poncho, compass, snack, bottle of water, cell phone, camera, weapon, and proper ammo. Of course I have to have a turkey vest with the right compartments and seat in it. I know, I know—a Butterball is much cheaper at the grocery store. However, I never got the rush of placing it in the cart like I do when I squeeze the trigger on my Remington 870 12-gauge at thirty yards!

I make sure I'm familiar with my weapon. I want to know it and my limitations. I know what shells pattern the best out of it and use those. I rarely step into the woods without someone with me anymore. I'm usually with one of my children, and we repeatedly go over safety precautions. If the weapon is unloaded, the chamber stays open, and the barrel is always pointed up or down—*never* in the direction of others. Chamber open or not, never point a weapon in the direction of another human being!

We often go to great lengths to prepare for whatever hobby or life event we're facing—well, most of them. There are two events in life that some of us do not think about much. One is death, and the other is judgment. In regard to death, if Jesus tarries at His second coming, all of you reading this book will die. It's certain "inasmuch as it is appointed for men to die once" (Hebrews 9:27). This tells us that all men and women have an appointment with death. It's fixed. It's on God's calendar, in His planner. He'll get an alert, so to speak. We don't know how or when, but it's fixed, and you won't be late.

The second part of Hebrews 9:27 reads, "And after this comes judgment." That means that our lives will be judged in accordance with how we have lived. There are two types of people at two different versions of judgment. One is the "great white throne" judgment. This is where the devil, his demons, and all the people who rejected Jesus as their Lord and Savior will be cast into the lake of fire. This is eternal. Once you're in hell, there's no hope of ever getting out. When a person has been there ten trillion years, it will be like a millisecond because it will be an eternity. These people weren't prepared to meet God.

The other people will be at the judgment's seat of Christ. They have trusted Christ as their Savior. Their works will be judged, and they will receive their rewards based on what they did with the lives Christ gave them. Some of them will be heavily rewarded, and some not as much because of how they squandered what they had been given in Christ.

Can a person prepare to meet God? Why do people put it off? Are you prepared? How does a person prepare to meet Him?

The answer to the first question is yes, a person can prepare to meet God! We should make sure this is in place before doing anything else. It's of utmost importance. It's a matter of urgency!

This is something you do not need to put off. Some put this off out of sheer busyness. They have so much going on they just plan to get around to it. Many never get there. Some put it off out of fear that they will have to give up some sinful pleasure that they enjoy. I hear of many who want to wait until they've partied a little longer or until they're older. However, that time may never come. As we grow older and have resisted the Holy Spirit, we become hardened to the good news. So are you prepared? I don't mean "maybe" or "I think so." I mean, do you *know* that you're prepared to meet the God of the universe and enter heaven on His terms?

You can. Here's how it works. Humanity has a problem. That problem is sin. Sin means to miss the mark. It's the picture of an archer aiming at a target and missing it altogether. You see, God has laws, and we've broken them. Sin marred the human race in the garden of Eden with the first man and woman. Adam and Eve were in the garden, and Adam had been instructed that he could eat from all trees in the garden except for one.

Eve was deceived by the serpent, who was the devil, into thinking it would make her wise. "When the women saw that the tree was good for food, and that it was a delight to the eyes and that the tree was desirable to make one wise, she took from its fruit and ate; and she gave also to her husband with her and he ate" (Genesis 3:6). This poses a huge problem for the human race. God called this act of rebellion sin, and the consequences were great!

Romans 5:12 informs us, "Therefore, just as through one man sin entered into the world, and death through sin, and so death spread to all men, because all sinned." Because of what happened in the garden, we all are born guilty, with a sin nature. We have a bent toward sin. Our flesh craves it and cannot keep God's law perfectly. Romans 3:23 states, "For all have sinned and fall short of the glory of God."

We are all lawbreakers. If you break the law, you will suffer the consequences—that is, if you're caught. God sees all, hears all, and knows all your thoughts and everything there is to know about you. I once met a man who said he was not a sinner. I asked him if he had ever told a lie. He pondered that for a moment and said, "I don't believe I have." Wow! He didn't live in reality. Of course he has lied. He did that day again when he was talking to me. God's penalty for breaking the law is to end up at The Great White Throne Judgment. Remember that. Because we are sinners by nature and choice, we deserve to go to hell. If we all got what we deserved, that would be where we'd spend eternity. Thankfully the story doesn't end there.

Romans 5:8 tells us, "But God demonstrates His own love toward us in that while we were yet sinners Christ died for us." God placed His Son in the womb of a virgin. There was no natural process of conception, so He was not born with a sinful nature. He had the nature of His heavenly Father. He grew up in a carpenter's home with brothers and sisters. He never sinned. Did you get that? He never lied, looked at a woman with lust in his heart, wanted something that did not belong to Him, and so on. Perfection! This is an important fact, because if He had committed one act of sin, His death on the cross would be worthless to us.

Because he was sinless, He could be the sacrificial lamb for our sins. He was beaten, spit on, made fun of, stripped, scourged, had tufts of his beard pulled out, and was nailed to a cross. His blood was shed. That was the payment for our sin debt. He paid a debt that we owed and could not pay. First Corinthians 15:3–4 communicates this truth: "Christ died for our sins according to the Scriptures, and that He was buried, and He was raised on the third day according to the Scriptures." Romans 4:25 explains it this way: "He who was delivered over because of our transgressions, and was raised because of our justification." The resurrection makes it possible for us to be made right with God. This is not automatic. Humanity's problem is sin, and God's provision is Christ. The process of receiving Him is next.

As stated earlier, Jesus's death on the cross doesn't mean that all people will be saved. People must repent and believe in Christ, and Jesus said so Himself. In Mark 1:15 Jesus said, "The time is fulfilled the Kingdom of Heaven is at hand; repent and believe in the gospel." The word *repent* means "to have a change of mind, that is a heartfelt sorrow for the course pursued," and a person must be willing to turn from that pattern. You must say, "God, I know I'm a sinner. I've broken Your law, and I'm sorry. I want to turn from my sin." Then a person must believe that Jesus died on the cross for our sins and that He was buried and raised. When people do this, God sends the Holy Spirit to live inside them, and they begin the journey of following Jesus. What a glorious day that is! Oh, by the way—this is what prepares you to meet God.

Before you move on to the next chapter, think about these questions. Are you ready? Are you sure? Why not stop now and make sure? Maybe you're sure but are walking at a guilty distance from the Lord. Will you return? I hope so! I'm praying for you! Don't put it off; be prepared!

Chapter 2

Being Thankful

In the midnineties I was hunting and filming for Drury Outdoors. It was an incredible privilege that many desired to do but few ever did. I was blessed with the opportunity.

I was hunting in my hometown with a good friend. He was running the camera that day. This was the first year we'd hunted this particular property and only our second time being there. It was flat river-bottom timber not far from the Mississippi River. I was about twenty-three years old and a brand-new believer. My whole world was changing from a tough, foulmouthed young man to a person who was desperately trying to follow Christ. I was really rough around the edges. God's grace is sufficient to change and grow us.

We went to the stand for an evening hunt. We used API tree strands, the kind with the small platform that strapped on to the tree, and we used the T-bolt system that came with it to secure the stand. Generally, we screwed steps into the tree and ended up about twenty feet in the air.

It was a clear, sunny afternoon in late October. I was shooting a Browning Mirage with a five-inch overdraw. My arrows were 2013 shafts with feather fletching and a one-hundred-grain four-blade Muzzy broadhead. I liked those because of the big chisel point on the tip. The guys we were filming for wanted us to shoot pretty much anything that walked by. We had a doe, and then a small year-and-a-half-old buck walked through.

It was close to that time when you're on high alert. You know what I'm talking about—the light begins to dim, and the bigger bucks like to move. We spotted a deer about eighty to ninety yards behind us. This was definitely out of bow range. It was a little windy that afternoon. I tried to grunt at this deer, but he didn't hear me.

Our stands were positioned right in the flow of whitetail traffic. That was evident by the game that had already passed by. I grunted louder and louder. He was coming our way. During his journey toward us, he stopped and drank. He looked like he was about 130 inches. He was an 8-pointer with about a sixteen-inch inside spread. Yes, I was a bit nervous at this point. I had an arrow knocked with my bow hanging up next to me. I put my grunt call inside my coat, so I didn't take a chance on it hanging up on my bow string. I grabbed my bow, fastened my rope release onto the string, and put enough tension on it to hold it in place. I waited.

He stopped at twenty-five yards on the other side of the tree and looked around. My heart pounded out of my chest. I was thinking, *Come on, come on, come on!* He began to walk again. I drew my bow and waited for him to hit the opening I'd picked out to shoot him. It was roughly twenty yards away. He was walking at a pretty good pace by now, and when he hit the opening, I let an arrow fly. I was shooting about three hundred feet per second. He took off with his tail tucked. I knew my shot placement was not the best. I'd been aiming where I needed to, but in the heat of the battle I did not swing my bow follow-through with the deer's walking pattern or stop him in the opening. He was walking from my left to right. I saw him lie down about eighty yards away. When some other deer came by him, he got up and went with the other deer. We watched the footage and said, "Yep, gut shot!"

We chose to wait until morning to go find him. I hated to do that, but at this point it was the best thing to do. The footage was great. He was a nice buck. It was just a mistake on my part to not stop him with my voice or a call to get a quick, steady shot. By the way, this is a practice that I started doing and continue to do today. We had to find him. It was a long night for me! This was my first buck kill on video, and it would be on a production. It also meant income for us as well, as we were compensated for kills and recovery on video. Daylight could not come soon enough for me and my buddy Herb. We made sure we marked the last place we saw him lie down before he took off across an open field to another clump of trees.

Shortly after daylight we were back at our stands and did a short interview where the arrow was stuck in the ground. We followed the blood trail. It dried up. We walked across the field to the trees, roughly a narrow four-acre patch. We had talked about the wind direction the night before and thought that maybe he would have kept the wind to his back and relied on his eyesight to look for predators in front of him.

So we moved slowly through the timber. It was getting thicker. There weren't any more signs. I was hoping we were going to find this deer. We kept walking slowly. At this point doubt was creeping in, especially if he had moved beyond this patch of woods. Then I saw a patch of brown in the distance. As I got closer, I saw antlers and knew this was the deer I'd shot the night before. I was excited and thankful! We did our interview and loaded him up. By the way, he only measured 110 inches. I tend to big eye them a little on the hoof…

Let's talk about being thankful. It's a continual admonition throughout the Bible. First Thessalonians 5:18 reads, "In everything give thanks." Ephesians 5:20 tells us, "Always giving thanks for all things in the name of our Lord Jesus Christ." These are just two of numerous examples.

Let's take a few minutes to look at them further. Paul is writing to the church in Thessalonica, and he is writing to strengthen their faith and assure them of Christ's return for them. When he says, "In everything give thanks," He wants us to find ourselves with a thankful attitude in all situations. When a situation that is less than favorable presents itself, we face the temptation to complain rather than be thankful. We can always find something to be thankful for in difficult times. How about the simple fact that as believers, no matter how rough things get, we are still going to heaven when we die? That alone should make us want to shout with joy! We have to look beyond what's going on and see the end result. This will help us be thankful.

Let's just say I was discouraged about putting a bad shot on that deer. If we just dwelt on that alone, we would have been in bad shape. But as a believer, I can pull back and be thankful for so much, such as my health, family, the privilege to hunt, the ability to climb a tree—not to mention my salvation, the church, His word, and the like. You see what I mean? If we always pull back and look at the situation with a biblical worldview, it's not hard to be thankful. It's a choice. That's right—your situation does not make you stressed or unthankful. You and I make a conscious choice to be that way. Let that sink in for a moment. Read it again. We *choose* not to be thankful. That's tough medicine to swallow, but it's true. It's like a dose of Kaopectate—chalky and nasty (my mom made me drink that stuff when I was a kid, which I jokingly say equals child abuse!). It's still true.

I don't mean to make your situation sound petty, because you may be dealing with some tough stuff right now, the kind of stuff where all you can do is put one foot in front of the other and move forward. Or you're so paralyzed, you don't know how you'll move forward. Jesus will help you. Lean on Him, cry out to Him, and ask Him to give you a thankful heart in the midst of the storm. The song by Casting Crowns is perfect for your situation: "I Will Praise You in This Storm."

Let's ratchet this up a notch or two. What we are about to discuss is not milk to sip but meat to chew. In the second passage, it says, "Always giving thanks for all things." Paul is writing to the church in Ephesus from prison. Let me say that again. He is writing from prison! He said to be thankful *for* all things. Now let's wade out here slowly and feel our way through this. It's kind of like trout fishing in deeper water. If you can't see the bottom, you proceed slowly, with caution. What Paul is commanding here (yes, it's a command) comes after the command to be filled with the Holy Spirit. Thankful people are filled with the Spirit of God. This order is given in the plural form, which means it's for every believer. It's also in the passive voice, which means the object of the filling is to be yielded. Finally, it's given in the present tense, which means it should be ongoing throughout one's life. This can only come by confession of sin, yielding, and asking God to fill you. This is a moment-by-moment need for us.

The only way you can be thankful for all things is to be filled with the Holy Spirit, period! That's the starting point. However, as we wade out a little deeper, we realize God allows everything in our lives. Nothing takes Him by surprise. The devil does not have free reign to do as he pleases; he has to have God's permission. So if we look at every circumstance through the lens God has given us to accomplish His purpose, although we may not fully understand it in our lifetime, we can be thankful for it. I told you this was meat. It may be tough steak right now, but keep chewing—don't spit it out just yet.

I know about a woman who is confined to a wheelchair because of a freak diving accident in her teen years. She is now a senior adult and a quadriplegic. She has a radio program, has written books, and has ministered to thousands around the world; because of her accident, she gained the right perspective. Today she is thankful for all God has done because of her accident. God's purposes were accomplished through her trial.

I know there are a lot of horrible things that happen. Let us not forget that they happen because we live in a fallen, sinful, broken world with messed-up people. However, we can trust Romans 8:28, "And we know that God causes all things to work together for good to those who love God, to those who are called according to his purpose."

As we continue to wade out in the stream, let me suggest that we can be thankful for all things. I've had some difficult experiences. I got my jaw broken. I was thrown head first into the bumper of a truck by a man I grew up with in my neighborhood. My mouth was wired shut for six weeks, I lost weight, I would not be able to play college football that fall, and I paid for the surgery out of my own pocket. While I would not like to repeat the experience, *I thank God for it*. It has taught me much about forgiveness and perseverance in difficult times.

So you see, you and I can be thankful for all things if we gain God's perspective. Would I have been thankful if I hadn't found the 8-pointer? Yes, eventually, once I gained His perspective.

What about you? Are you going through a rough time? What do you need to be thankful for at this time? Ask God to help you. I know He will!

Chapter 3

Dealing with Discouragement and Disappointment

It was a cool November afternoon during the shotgun deer season in Pike County, Illinois. I hadn't harvested a deer yet. I was at a friend's house in his driveway, talking about the morning hunt, new strategies, and plans for the evening hunt. It was the last day of gun season, and usually on the last day, guys made a big push or drive and position guys where they might get a shot at the deer that came running by. I've been involved with this kind of hunting, and it's been fruitful in the past. There are antlers mounted in my office right now to prove it. The folks who owned a big chunk of land south of his house were about to make a drive. We didn't hunt with them and didn't know what was about to happen.

As we stood there, I saw a *huge* 10-pointer run out of the woods from their block of timber, cross the gravel road, and jump the fence into an open pasture! He was a brute! I guessed he would have scored in the 160s. I was about twenty and in decent shape. At this time I was not a believer in Jesus. The buck was now on property where I had permission to hunt. He was headed for a block of timber I'd been bow hunting. I knew he would slow down when he got inside the woods, cruise up through that patch, and cross over onto another landowner, where I also had permission to hunt. I jumped in the truck and drove down to that farm, devising a plan in my mind of how to get into position to get a shot at this big whitetail.

I jumped out of my Chevy S-10 pickup and loaded my Remington 870 with three three-inch slugs. I had a Tasco 3-9x40 mm scope on it. I had to run up a hill that was close to a sixty-degree incline for about sixty yards. It had been raining, the ground was wet, and that good, rich, Midwestern black dirt was soft. My adrenaline was pumping. I did not have any time to waste to be where I thought I needed to be in order to have a chance at a shot.

I came to the fence I had to cross to reach the patch of timber we'd watched him enter. The field was sown in winter wheat that was about three inches tall. The ground was soft. I was sinking about three inches per step as I jogged to where I needed to be in order to spot him. I thought it would be better to run around the south end of the woods and slip in about halfway down the hill.

I was puffing like a freight train at this point. It's amazing what we'll do to try to harvest one of these big boys. I slowly and cautiously stepped into the woods, scanning the area for this buck. I was trying not to breathe loudly. I looked down the hill where he'd come in and slowly looked up through the woods. With all the leaves gone, it's easy to spot deer when they're moving.

As I got even with where I was in relation to looking across the timber, boom! There he was. He was about a hundred yards away. With a .270 this would have been an easy shot. With my slug gun, it would be a bit more challenging. I stood up, free-handing my weapon, trying to find him in my scope. I harvested a doe one time at about 125 on the fly with this weapon, so I knew it could be done. I found him. I was breathing so hard from the run and shaking from having a little buck fever; it was hard to get settled in on him. My gun barrel was going up and down like a bobber in the springtime catching bluegill. (I know you've never had this problem before, right?)

I took the safety off, held my breath, zeroed in on my target, and fired! I know you're not really supposed to hold your breath, but I had to due to the intensity of the moment. I hit him! He jumped and hunched up, tucked his tail, and slowly ran off through the timber. Twenty-five-plus years later I can still see the image in my mind.

I began to trail him right away. Bright red blood, but not a lot. It did appear that I got at least one lung. I was concerned but kept forging ahead. I tracked him through the wheat field. He was sinking deep as he crossed there. He would have probably dressed about 200 or 225 pounds. So on the hoof you can add another fifty to that weight. He had the strength to get over the fence, which was a four foot woven wire fence with two strands of barbed wire on it. This was probably ten to fourteen minutes after I shot him. Knowing what I know now about deer that are hit in the spleen, liver, lung, or the guts, I would have stopped and waited about three hours.

I climbed the fence and tracked him about forty yards across a pasture and into a block of timber. He was bedded down and jumped up and ran slowly. There was not a tremendous amount of blood in the bed. However, I knew he would die eventually. I could not get a shot at him because the woods were too thick. This particular tract of land had three little fingers of timber on it, with open field surrounding it. I'd shot my first two deer with a bow on this property. I was concerned that he would get over on another landowner who was not friendly to any other hunters and would not give permission to get in there and track him, especially if he knew it was a good catch. If the buck crossed the property line, he was as good as gone. He was about a hundred yards from that fence.

I had a hunch he was in that last little finger of timber by now. I went to it with hopes of getting a final shot. I jumped him again when I stepped into the woods. All I could see was his massive rack walking about seventy-five yards away. I thought I would just quickly step out and around that block of timber and shoot him before he crossed the fence. So I did. I had my gun up on my shoulder with the barrel at about a forty-five-degree angle, ready to raise and shoot as I kept alert and was steadily walking. He did not show up. It was as if he just vaporized. He was not in the finger. He was not in the pasture. He was nowhere to be found. He also had stopped bleeding.

I was sick to my stomach. To this day I don't know where he went.

I looked for him for a couple of days, to no avail. It was a sad day for me. You hunters who have experienced this know what I mean. I was so distraught that I did not gun-hunt for three or four years. I only bow hunted in the future. I was one disappointed young man. I'd made several mistakes and knew I was responsible for the outcome, and I wished I could go back and do it over one more time.

Life is full of disappointing moments. Our natural tendencies in the flesh lean toward discouragement. We do and think all kinds of self-defacing things. We're capable of even slipping into depression because of discouragement and disappointment.

We'll all be disappointed at certain times and in particular seasons in our lives. We need to be grounded in the Bible to fight discouragement. It's our weapon in times of spiritual warfare. It's called the sword of the Spirit, and it's sharper than a two-edged sword. It's able to help you resist temptation. It's a comfort in our times of trouble. There are commands to obey and promises to claim in the Bible. When you're reading the Bible, you need to ask yourself which one it is. Is it a truth to claim or a command to obey? We demonstrate our love to God by obeying him. We get our hope from God's word by the promises He has given us.

In 2 Corinthians 4, we have some truths that are helpful in fighting discouragement. In verses 14 and 16 Paul writes, "knowing that He who raised the Lord Jesus will raise us also with Jesus and will present us with you … Therefore, we do not lose heart." We literally do not become discouraged. Paul wanted them to know that no matter what they were facing in this life, they could be encouraged by the fact that we will share in the resurrection. If we know the Lord Jesus as our Savior, this is a great promise. He will raise us on that great day to join our newly resurrected body with our spirit. What a glorious day that will be!

Meantime, here on earth, we face the temptation of being discouraged. Whether it's losing a big buck, not doing well on a test, losing a job, experiencing poor health, enduring the loss of a family member, and so forth, we all face difficult times of various kinds. However, no matter how bad it gets, it will be temporary.

The difficulty we have now is but for a moment. In verse 17 Paul continues, "For momentary, light affliction is producing for us an eternal weight of glory far beyond all comparison." Paul calls what we face momentary light affliction. Now if you know what he went through (see 2 Corinthians 11:23–28), you would say this guy is either nuts or has been changed by God's grace in such a way that he has a distinct eternal perspective. The latter is true. He was changed.

Sometimes when we are going through difficult, dark days, we can easily focus on the problem and not our Savior and the big picture. Doing this will lead us to discouragement. However, as we have been commanded in James 1:2, "Consider it all joy, my brethren, when you encounter various trials."

We are to do what? How in the world can we do this? By focusing on the outcome in verses 3–4: "Knowing that the testing of your faith produces endurance. And let endurance have its perfect result, so that you may be perfect and complete, lacking in nothing." So according to this passage, when my faith is being tested by trials, I should count it all as joy and focus on Jesus, by faith. This will produce endurance and maturity. Yes? That is what that passage is saying.

Now what will help you see the insanity of the request is that the people James was writing to were severely persecuted and scattered from their homeland after the stoning of Stephen in Acts 7. There was also a famine in the region. Talk about trials, huh? They were living in hard times, and they were commanded to "consider it all joy."

The command wouldn't be given if we didn't have the ability to carry it out. We do. Our human nature alone could not accomplish this task. It must be produced by the Holy Spirit now living within us. You and I have to make a choice. Will we obey scripture and be empowered to do so? Many wait for feeling instead of striking out in obedience. God will give the strength and grace as we obey Him. Try it and watch the Lord work!

Are you battling discouragement? Is there something in your life that you just can't seem to shake? Is it stealing your joy? Why not try to gain God's perspective? In light of eternity, we can consider it joy! Let it produce endurance and maturity in your life.

Chapter 4

Perseverance Pays Off

It was a very cool spring morning in south Alabama. I believe it was in 2012. The temperature was in the low forties. Turkey season was in full swing. I was hunting a farm about an hour north of where I was living at the time. Being in Central Standard Time meant an "early out" to get where I needed to be that morning.

I drove to the farm, unlocked the padlock, and drove back to the barn. I had about a half-mile walk to get where my buddy Eric told me he'd been seeing a gobbler. I got all my gear on, loaded my weapon, and headed down the road on foot. My weapon of choice to turkey hunt is an old Remington 870 Express 12 gauge that my parents bought me for my eighteenth birthday. Many a critter has come to the end of his days because of that gun. It's a good gun, but it's special to me because my folks bought it for me. You may have a weapon like that.

I found the spot where he'd been seeing the gobbler. There were two trees side by side in a field just off the road, which ran through his farm. I was there about twenty minutes before daylight. Perfect! I sat there and prayed, thinking about how good God has been to me. I was excited about the morning's hunt.

God's creation began to wake up. The sky lightened up a little, and the birds began to sing. This is my favorite time of day. I love to hoot and get the owls cranked up in hopes of getting a gobbler to fire off. Sure enough, I had a gobbler down in the holler sound off about thirty minutes after first light. He was getting cranked up on the limb. There's no sweeter sound in the spring woods than the gobble of an old tom. It seems to me, in Alabama, the turkeys stay on the limb a little longer than in other places I've hunted.

I was about to give a fly-down cackle when I heard a pickup truck driving down the farm road toward me. *What? Who in the world could this be?* I was not a happy camper. He drove by where I was set up and kept on going. The old tom went silent. Yep, his beak could not have been any tighter if you'd bailing wired it shut. So I sat and waited. In my twenties I probably would have gotten up and moved, but I'm a little more patient these days. I sat there for about thirty minutes and waited. I was wondering what was going to happen, and then boom! He gobbled. He was still in the tree. So I called to him and then set still. He gobbled again and was now on the ground.

I began working this turkey, and he steadily headed toward my direction. It helps to be in line with where he wants to go anyway. Setup is key. I saw him at about ninety yards cross out of the holler to a little patch of small trees in front of me. He had the thickest beard of any turkey I'd ever shot. You've probably heard the term "paintbrush beard." Well, he had one! That thing was thick! It bounced off his chest as he walked.

I raised my gun and rested it on my knee and pressed it against my shoulder. It was pointed in the direction I thought he might pop out of the woods. There he was, just like clockwork. He was right in front of me at about sixty yards, walking straight at me. He got to about thirty yards and made a forty-five-degree shift. He evidently thought the hens that were talking to him were beyond the next tree line (soft calling).

This shift poses a little bit of a problem. I shoot left handed, and he was now moving to my left and was walking fast (like one of those mall walkers with his britches pulled up way too high). He was going somewhere. He was about twenty-eight steps out.

I clucked to stop him and repositioned to get a quick shot. Bang! I rolled him! He flopped a couple of times and got up and took off running!

I'd been sitting in forty-degree weather for more than an hour, and I was in my early forties, so I was a little stoved up (stiff and unable to move well). I took off after him as hard as I could run. I ran about eighty to a hundred yards and came to a brush pile that sat out from the edge of the wood line about thirty yards or so. I stopped halfway between the wood line and the brush pile. I scanned the area, trying to spot him. The foliage was already fully grown, and I knew if he ran in the woods I may not get him.

All of a sudden I heard the strangest groaning or croaking noise from the direction of the brush pile. I snapped around and saw him shining in the sun next to the pile. I shouldered my gun and let one go, bang! He dropped and didn't go anywhere after that. I walked over to him—and wow, what a beard! Nice spurs too! His beard was as wide as the palm of my hand and just over eleven inches long. The spurs were roughly 1 3/8 inches long. A nice bird indeed.

As it turns out, the man who drove by in the truck was doing some dozer work on the back side of the property. All was well. I've thought many times if I had left that spot and gone somewhere else, I would have missed a great opportunity. I've also pondered the fact that if I hadn't immediately taken off in hot pursuit, I might have never found him. I don't like to injure an animal and not recover it. This has happened only a few times in my life. One was mentioned earlier in this book.

The word perseverance comes to mind. How many times have you heard a great story about someone persevering through great difficulty and seeing how it paid off? You could also use the word persistent. This reminds me of the story of the widow and the unjust judge in the Bible. In Luke 18, Jesus tells the story to encourage persistent prayer. There was a judge who "did not fear God or respect man" (verse 2). This widow kept asking him that she be given legal protection. He persisted in being unwilling, and she persisted in asking. In verse 5, he says, "Yet because this widow bothers me, I will give her legal protection, otherwise by continually coming she will wear me out." He basically said because this woman is wearing me out, I'm going to give her what she's asking for so she'll shut up! Her perseverance paid off.

Listen to what Jesus said in verses 7–8: "Now will not God bring about justice for his elect who cry to Him day and night, and will delay long over them? I tell you that He will bring about justice for them quickly. However, when the Son of Man comes will He find faith on the earth?" Jesus is teaching the importance of prevailing in prayer. He said if we come to him day and night, God won't delay. Protracted prayer, persistent prayer, with a persevering attitude of the heart will produce results when we pray. This is key to our prayer life. I'm under the conviction that if God leads me to pray for something, He wants it accomplished, so I'm not to quit until it comes. It may not come in my lifetime, but it will be done after I'm gone.

How often do we quit praying for someone or something because we don't see anything happening? I currently meet with a group of men to pray for more than one hundred men in our community to be saved. There are a few women on that prayer list. We've been meeting for almost two years now. Several people on that list have been saved or returned from a backslid condition. This has happened because anywhere from seven to fifteen men have gathered for fifteen months to pray for these people to get right with God, and it's happening. Don't you quit!

Who in your sphere of influence needs the Lord? Are you praying for them? Are you persistently bringing their names before God for them to be saved? If you're not doing that, you can always start today! Start a list, regularly gather with some friends, and pray for them. Watch God work in their lives. Do it with a persevering heart attitude. Cry out day and night, and believe that praying to God will work.

Chapter 5

Keep Your Word

THE NEXT SPRING I found myself winding down the season having not gone turkey hunting very much at all. I'd had a busy travel schedule preaching revivals and traveling. I always take the children at least one time. I took Josiah once, and I think one other time, but that was it. I was preaching a revival meeting at home the last week of the season. When I'm in the midst of a meeting, I do not feel like getting up at three thirty to go turkey hunting. But I'd promised John and Noel (two of my other children) that I would take them before the season was over. The season ended on Wednesday the thirtieth of April. This was Monday the twenty-eighth. I told them we would go the next morning, the twenty-ninth. I didn't want to go, but a promise is a promise.

I got home late that night. There was a chance of rain the next day. I was extremely exhausted after preaching. *I didn't want to go!*

Yep, you guessed it. When I woke that morning, we were having some light rain. I woke up my daughter Noel and John one of my sons. We got camoed up and grabbed some snacks. I loaded up on coffee, and away we went. They were both excited. I was less than thrilled, but I do love to turkey hunt; it just wasn't the best time for me.

We drove to the farm, unlocked the gate, and drove back to the barn. We had a good little walk to get where we needed to be. Once again my buddy told me he'd been seeing a bird with a really long beard in this spot. It was peppering rain. Just a sprinkle, but enough to soak you if you stayed out in it a while. We trudged along in the dark. They were elated to go turkey hunting with Dad! They love to go with me.

I got to the spot where we needed to set up. John was almost eight, and Noel was eleven. They were just going to observe. I looked and looked for a tree to set up against but couldn't find what I wanted. I finally settled on a pine that was only about seven inches in diameter. I put down some black plastic for the kids to sit on and had them sit on either side of the tree. By this time it was thirty minutes after first light, and we had not heard a gobble.

I slipped out into the field and put a decoy out at twenty-five yards from where the kids were sitting. I just had one hen decoy with me. Many times that's all I use. I hurried back to my spot, trying not to make any noise. I sat between the children and was coaching them. I'd been talking to them about how well a turkey could see and schooling them on what "don't move" meant if I said it. It has been suggested that a wild turkey's eyesight is twelve times better than our twenty-twenty vision. That means he can see a gnat raise his back leg to scratch his belly at forty yards.

As we got settled in, the rain continued to pepper down on us. It was a slow, steady sprinkle. Still nothing had gobbled. I had one knee up and the gun resting on it to be ready, just in case. I would call, casting my voice, in three different directions. I was using my diaphragm. I would wait about ten minutes before calling again.

The water had beaded up on my shotgun, and I'd just run my hand down the barrel to wipe it off. The decoy was out in front of us to the left. John was sitting on my left, and Noel was on my right. We had been sitting there for about thirty minutes or so. Nothing had gobbled so far. We were wet and cold, and I was beginning to think this was not going to produce a turkey.

I happened to catch a little movement out of my peripheral vision. I slowly turned my head to the right. At the edge of the field, roughly sixty yards away, stood a big gobbler. He was about a quarter strut. He was puffing up a little for the decoy. It was raining, and he wasn't interested in a show. He took a few steps toward the decoy and then looked our way, hard. I got really nervous. I already had the gun on him, and the safety was off. He turned toward the decoy and walked a few more steps. I noticed how long his beard looked, and I thought this was the one from the pictures we had on the trail camera. He reached the twenty-five-yard mark from the decoy and was about forty-three yards from us. He looked our way again. He stretched his neck high. I've seen this look dozens of times. Usually after this they set their wing feathers and run like the wind.

He saw something he didn't like. I didn't know what it could have been. Maybe it was the three humans in camo next to a single, skinny pine tree.

I had the bead of the gun on his head, and he began to set his wing feathers. He did not get that task finished. I touched off the trigger on top of the hill and kaboooom! It echoed down the hollow. He dropped like a rock. The kids were pumped to say the least! We high-fived! Their smiles stretched from ear to ear. That was well worth the early out and the rain-soaked bodies.

We ran over to the bird and contained him. He had dandy spurs and a very long beard. I'd killed turkeys up to that point that had 11 to 11 1/2-inch beards, but never 12. This bird had a 12 1/4-inch beard and 1 3/8-inch spurs! Now I was pumped! We took several pictures with this trophy bird. I was able to capture their smiles. We picked up our decoy and began to walk back to the truck, thanking God for how he had blessed us that morning. I was telling the story to them as I passed the spot where I bagged the one that almost got away, the one with the paintbrush beard that I'd killed the year before.

The Lord blessed my commitment to do what I said I would do. I kept my word. I told the kids I would take them. I'd wanted to sleep in—I was tired. But I wanted them to know Dad tries to do what he says he'll do. Let your yeses be yes and your nos be no. Ephesians 4:15 says, "Speaking the truth in love." We are to express the truth in love and action. We know that the Bible says we "should not lie." The book of Ephesians later says in 6:4: "And, Fathers, do not provoke your children to anger." One of the ways we as parents can provoke our children to anger is by not keeping our word. I try to be careful to fulfill what I say I'll do, which means I have to be careful about what I tell them in the first place.

That sounds simple, right? If you have children or grandchildren, they're going to learn integrity from you. They'll do what you do most of the time, especially when they get older. Notice I said do what you *do*! What we *say* is worthless if it doesn't match our actions. How many promises have you made to your children this year? Are you working on fulfilling them? "Son, we'll go to the game." "Son, we'll go to the park and throw the football." "Sweetie, we'll go on a date." "I'll play dolls with you later today."

Yes, I did just say that! When we do not fulfill these promises, we could add to the anger and resentment that builds up inside children. I have not kept my promises 100 percent of the time, but when I don't, which is few and far between, I go to them, confess, and ask their forgiveness. I want them to know what it means to have integrity.

How about in other relationships? Do you tell people you'll pray for them and then don't? Do you tell someone you'll do something and then don't do it? Do you return phone calls, texts, e-mails, and so on, when something is needed or being asked of you?

This all comes down to being dependable. I hope you do what you say you'll do. If you don't, you can start today. Sometimes this happens with our spouse. There's no more important relationship than the one you have with your spouse. By all means we need to keep our word with that special person God has given us.

Maybe you need to put this book down and go get your relationship right with someone. If the Lord is convicting you now and someone has come to mind, this is how you approach that person. You say, "God has convicted me that I have not kept my word to you." Then state what it is. Ask for forgiveness. Express your grief, and then pledge to do better.

If it's with your children, engage your spouse to help you. This is how I do this: I simply tell my wife that I've promised the kids I will do "x" with them. Then I ask her to help me not to forget. She won't! She remembers these things and helps me. Women naturally work at keeping Dad engaged with the children. By the way, the fruit of this will be good. You reap what you sow!

Chapter 6

Follow the Rules

It was a cold, snowy morning in the Midwest. I was headed to the goose blind that morning. I was hunting with three federal game wardens that day and one older man of seventy-six. It had snowed about five inches the night before. This meant that in order for our decoys to look authentic, we were going to have to brush all the snow off them. It was going to be one of those overcast days that are perfect for shooting water fowl. Duck season had just closed a few days before this hunt.

I arrived early and began to brush off the decoys. We had about four hundred set out. About the time it started getting light, I was finished, and we were in the blind. We were anticipating a good morning. I was once again carrying my old 870. This gun has killed more game than any other gun I have owned. It's my favorite gun. I shoot skeet, turkeys, and doves with it.

About twenty-five mallards circled and landed right in front of us. They sat on the water for about thirty seconds and then got spooked and flew off. They were twenty yards from the blind.

The game warden on my left said to the one on the right, "What would you have done if I'd jumped up and started shooting those mallards?"

I didn't like his response. He said, "I would have hit Ronnie, because I would have figured you knew better." Ha-ha-ha! Not funny!

It was one of those mornings when there was little or no wind.

Some giant Canadian geese came toward us. They were a long way out, but they were low. It appeared like they were headed right for us, so we all began to call. I was running a Double Cluck Plus by Knight and Hale. It's my favorite goose call. We were all honking our brains out, and they were headed right at us. There were twelve or so in this bunch.

When they got close, someone yelled, "Get 'em, boys!"

We all jumped up and cut it into them. Several hit the ground. One had a band on his foot, and one had a band around his neck. The bands are a trophy for the waterfowler. I just knew I'd shot one, but as it turns out the game wardens swore they'd shot them. I didn't say anything. I didn't care. Well, maybe a little. We sat there and replayed the event again and again. You know hunters. We like to talk about our hunts.

We sat there for a while, and another bunch of giants came heading right for us! They were coming from the same direction the last bunch had come from. We began to call and plead with them to head to our little waterhole, with a nice field behind us full of goose decoys. They came in as if we were pulling them in on a string. You couldn't have asked for anything better.

When they got on top of us, we raised up and cut into them. They began to fall. It gets a little tricky at this point. You have to make sure you don't kill too many, especially if you're hunting with game wardens. What do you know—once we tallied them up, we had just enough for everyone to get their limit!

The wind picked up. I took my geese home and picked them in my shed—cold and no hot water, big mistake. However, I persevered and got them cleaned and ready to eat. It was a fun day!

When the game warden is watching, you'd better follow the rules. But there is someone greater than the game warden watching. You may fool the game warden, but you won't fool this warden. God knows what we do, when we do it, and how it gets done. He never misses anything, whether it's cheating on our taxes, catching too many fish, killing too many turkeys, hunting out of season, or looking at stuff on the Internet that we're not supposed to look at.

I could go on and on. None of us have been totally innocent in all these areas, I'm sure. Maybe you have, and you're one of the few. If that's the case, great job! Keep it up.

When I was a young man, I would break some game rules. I sat in a revival conference in North Carolina in 2000. The man who was preaching was telling a story about being in a church that was doing an eight-day revival meeting. All week long he sensed there were two men who needed to deal with something.

On the eighth day, which happened to be Sunday, after the service he got his food and sat at the table between these two men and said, "Okay, boys, what's wrong?" Nothing like beating around the bush, huh?

The men asked what he meant.

He said, "All week you've been under conviction and refusing to deal with something. Now out with it. What is it?"

They said if they did what he suggested in one of his messages, in order for them to clear their conscience, they would be thrown in jail. He quizzed them on what it was. They said they had numerous wild-game violations. They could not confess them.

He urged them to do so and said it was a small price to pay to be right with God. When he finished his message, I sat there, stunned. I couldn't move. I sensed that I needed to write down all my past wild-game violations, acts of vandalism, thievery, and so forth. and make them right. Most of these things happened before I got saved. I knew the Lord had forgiven me, but I needed to make restitution. So I began to write a long list of everything the Lord brought to my mind. I called one of my mentors in the faith and asked for his counsel. He encouraged me to follow through.

I began the process of calling the people on my list. One of the calls was to the mother of a man I'd gone to school with. I called her at work. I didn't know how else to get hold of her. I was 850 miles from home attending Bible college at the time. I confessed that I'd vandalized her son's truck, which was their truck, actually, when he had left it parked at the school for a ball game. I told her I was prepared to pay restitution on whatever the damages had been.

She was a believer and was overjoyed at the phone call. She would not let me pay her a dime. I asked for her forgiveness, and she was glad to grant it. She was so pleased to hear that I'd gotten saved.

I remember another instance that I had to set right. This may speak to the hunters reading this book. I was about nineteen and was turkey hunting with a friend early one morning. We were trespassing. Once we got in the woods, we split up. I heard a bird gobbling. I would hoot, and he would answer. I kept hooting, and he kept gobbling.

The landowner and one of his brothers rarely ever turkey hunted, but I heard them pull in and get out of their truck. They entered the woods and began to hoot. The gobbler answered them. In order to get away from them, I had to move toward the turkey. Eventually, I ended up right underneath him.

I had a decision to make. I could just run off and keep going back toward my friend's house through the woods or shoot the bird and then run back across two properties to his house. *I by no means am proud of what I did, nor do I do this kind of thing anymore.* I made the wrong choice to shoot the bird off the roost and pick him up and run! So I did.

The landowners began to holler and run after me. However, there was no way they were going to catch me. I weighed about 175 and was in tip-top shape. I ran until I got back to my friend's house.

So I had to call this landowner, confess, and ask for his forgiveness. I told him how I'd gotten saved about three years after that and how God wanted me to get things right with people. He graciously forgave me.

I had to call several others, but the most difficult was one of the game wardens I used to hunt with. He had recently become a believer as well. I had a long list of wild-game violations, and I knew I needed to call and confess every one of them. I'd shot stuff out of season, had trespassed, and had shot something and tagged it with someone else's tag. You get the picture, right? The Lord brought something to my mind that I hadn't written down while talking to him, and I was able to tell him about that as well. This all happened several years ago. After two years, if there were any complaints, they were thrown out. He told me I'd done the right thing by dealing with this. I assured him I did not knowingly break the law anymore. He was very gracious.

I have discovered that my integrity has become worth more to me than breaking the law. Romans 13 tells me that I am to be a man under authority. As long as the law does not require me to break God's law, I am to comply and obey. When I break the law of the land, I'm in violation of the principle that is laid out in this chapter. This is often overlooked in areas of speed limits, game limits, regulations, and so on. I confess that the speed limit still gets me every once in a while. It's important for us to do the right thing and obey the law. We need to respect and obey authority. If we don't, it's inadvertently disobedience toward God with consequences to come.

Maybe there are some things the Lord will require you to clear your conscience over. I trust you'll be sensitive to the Holy Spirit. Maybe you need to put this book down, get a pen and some paper, and write down some names that you need to contact. I hope and pray you'll be obedient.

Chapter 7

Studying Can Pay Off

WHETHER YOU WANT TO go out and find a spot to hang a deer stand or locate a flock of turkeys, you have to study the land. You have to find the animals you're looking to harvest. You need to learn their patterns of travel, where they like to bed down or roost, and where they like to feed and get a drink. These are important things that require us to get into the woods and study—or, to use a term you may be more familiar with, scout.

One time I was working for an outdoor company and was with the owner. We were in southeast Kansas. He was bow hunting, and I was filming. He had to go on a business trip for a couple of days in Denver, Colorado. He wanted me to stay, scout the property, and hang a couple of stands in a prime spot so we could get an opportunity to harvest a trophy buck. He left, and I began to scout around the properties on which we had permission to hunt. There was a lot of deer on these farms. My boss was becoming very well known nationwide at this time for his hunting ability. I wanted to find the right spot for him to get a good buck.

When you're hunting and filming, you have to take into consideration that you have two stands to hang and a camera arm. At that time in the midnineties, we were using a Panasonic 455 that shot footage on an S-VHS tape. We used the API Alumi-Lock tree stands as well as screw-in steps. So as I scouted, I would carry two stands, twenty steps, and a camera arm with a chain and binder to have in case I found *the spot*.

I walked into this patch of timber in the bottomland. Everything was pretty flat. There was a small hill to the right of where I was standing. I walked up to a ditch that didn't have any water in it, and I came across a trail that looked like a bunch of hogs had been running through. There were no wild hogs in southeast Kansas. This was deer traffic. Bingo!

I'd already gotten the forecast for the wind direction for the next few days. With that in mind, I began looking for the right spot. Where I needed to hang the stand because of deer activity and wind direction ended up being in a hackberry tree that was about ten to twelve inches in diameter. I began screwing in steps. Usually with ten steps I would be at the twenty-foot mark. I would tie off on my safety belt and pull my stand up after I'd screwed my tee bolt in for the stand to rest on.

I pulled the stand up and set it in place. I ran the strap around the tree, fastened it, and climbed onto the stand. To make sure it was secure, I would bounce around a little. You must make sure you're careful. There are too many hunting accidents each year that leave people paralyzed and sometimes dead.

I would then pull up the other stand and hang it ninety degrees to the back side of the hunter stand from where the deer activity would be. This usually gave me a great video angle. Once this stand was in place, I climbed up on it and pulled the chain, binder, and the metal block that our camera arm would fit on. I positioned it between me and the hunter stand. The arm is usually about a foot above the hunter's head while he's standing. I'd done this enough by this point in my journey that this process only took a few minutes. I would then set in both stands, see what needed to be trimmed for shooting lanes for the hunter, and decide what would give me optimum video capability. I loved being a producer in the woods. I had a lot of fun doing this. It was a game to me. I would study, study, study! Scout, scout, scout!

As I waited for my boss to get back into town, it began to rain and rain and rain some more. It rained for several days. We couldn't get the camera equipment wet or it would shut down on us. So we waited. Finally, the rain stopped.

We headed to the spot one afternoon for an evening hunt. When we got to the ditch right beside the tree where our set was hung, we found it full of water. It was a flowing little creek now! We climbed in. I was telling him about all the deer in the area that I saw and pointed out the "hog trail" full of deer tracks. It was fifteen yards from the stand. No way he would miss from this spot. We sat there with great anticipation. We had a doe and a small year-and-a-half-old buck come through that evening. He sure was giving me a hard time about that being such a great spot! I told him we could move if he wanted!

He chuckled and said, "No, we'll stay." He was just picking at me, which is something he loved to do.

We went back the next morning and had not seen a deer for a couple of hours.

My friend Mark slowly stood up and said, "Deer, deer, deer."

I looked over his shoulder and saw a doe headed for us. I said, "I see the doe."

He said, "No, buck, big buck!"

I looked behind the doe. At about fifty yards was a massive 10-pointer. I'm guessing he would go about 165 inches. Nice buck! They continued toward us. There was a small 6-point that came off the hill behind us, and the big buck snort-wheezed at him as soon as he saw him. It scared the daylights out of me. I'd never heard that in the woods before. It scared the little buck too! He took off out of there in a hurry. That was big boy's alert, saying "I'm about to whip your tail if you don't get out of here!"

The doe kept walking, and it appeared as if she was going to cross that big trail right in front of us. By that time I'd had about two minutes and thirty seconds of this buck. She crossed at fourteen yards right in front of us. When she got through the water, it was a few inches below her belly. The buck followed suit! When he got to the water, I knew he was as good as gone!

Mark let an arrow fly, and the buck bounced out of the water.

The footage was incredible. The buck jumped up on the bank and just stood there and looked around. Then he flicked his tail and seemed fine. I looked over my camera and saw Mark with a horrible look on his face. I knew then he had missed the buck.

The buck circled wide around us to catch up with the doe. It was a sad day and a sick feeling. We discovered that Mark had a bent arrow in his quiver and had forgotten. It was the arrow he'd knocked that morning. He was heartsick!

We moved the stands a couple hundred feet due to a wind change for the next couple of days. By this point we were eleven or twelve days into this trip. I had to hang my stand twenty-six feet in the air due to the tree's curvature. We saw a buck move across the top of the hill in front of us into a bedding thicket.

Mark said, "Do you think I should rattle?"

I said, "If it were me, I would."

He smashed the horns together for a rattling sequence that lasted about one minute. About two minutes after that, we saw the same buck coming out of the bedding area. He was looking for the buck fight! He walked about thirty yards from my hunting partner. I actually filmed him standing up in the same frame as this bruiser was walking by; he was a five by five, tight and tall. He probably would have scored in the 140s. He circled us to get downwind. There wasn't any noticeable wind that day. A faint movement of air was casting our scent right behind us.

The deer was six yards from the base of my tree. He stopped when he hit my wind and looked up. He was staring into the lens of the camera. He had picked me off at twenty-six feet! Unbelievable!

Mark was at full draw. The deer was quartering toward him; he would never take a "quartering to" shot. He thought the deer would turn slowly and he would get a shot as he turned. His first movement was a bolt of about fifteen to twenty yards. This put him in the brush. Mark let an arrow fly, and I heard tink, tink, tink, tink, tink as the arrow slapped off the trees, missing the deer.

Mark was devastated. Our hunt was over. It was time to pack up and head home. It was a long ride back to Missouri.

As I think about all the buck activity we experienced, I know it was due to several days of scouting and studying the land to put the set in the best spot possible. It took hours of walking, looking, and observing the sign left by the deer.

Second Timothy 2:15 says, "Be diligent to present yourself approved to God as a workman who does not need to be ashamed, accurately handling the word of truth." Study is important for men when it comes to the Bible. You need to study if you're going to lead your family in devotion and train your children in the discipline and instruction of the Lord (Ephesians 6:4). You can't give out what you don't know, and you don't know what you don't take the time to put into your mind and heart.

As men one day, we will stand before God and give an account for how we led our families. We must develop a biblical worldview and live life through that filter. What does it mean to have a biblical worldview? It means you view all of life through the lens of what the Bible teaches on how to live. So we get our basis of morality, ethics, integrity, and practice in all areas of life from the Bible. You may be thinking, *The Bible certainly does not have an answer for all of these areas of life.* You may be surprised. There is a principle to follow in areas where there are not direct commands to obey in all these areas.

We should study the word in such a way to ask the question that was asked in Charles Sheldon's classic book, *In His Steps:* "What would Jesus do?" What would happen in your life if you asked that question before you did anything? I mean it—every thought you allow to stay in your mind, every attitude, every spoken word, every dollar spent, everything you put on your calendar, every hour spent. If we did this, it would cause a radical shift in many areas of our lives. I believe is what the Lord wants from us. It will not come if we do not study the word of God. You can't know what He wants if you don't put the word in your mind and heart.

Stop for a moment and just ponder this ...

Did the Holy Spirit of God prompt you in any area? The Bible is for more than just reading; it's to be lived out. The world around us needs to see an incarnational picture of the Bible. In essence, it's the Bible with flesh. That is you and me living out the truth in our everyday lives.

The question is, how do you study? Well, I want to briefly cover three things:

1. The Bible must be studied in context. What does that mean? There was an original author, writing to an original reader. There were things going on during that period, time, and culture that have to be discovered to make sure we get the right meaning of the text. Why is this important? For example, in the New Testament's book of James, it was written approximately AD 44. Stephen had just been stoned, the people were scattered, and there was a famine in the land. Then he writes in chapter 1:2, "Consider it all joy my brethren when you encounter various trials." Now does that add to the meaning of what he says by knowing what's going on? It sure does for me!
2. It's best to study whole books of the bible to get the fuller meaning of a passage. This is where it's good to have a good study Bible with a lot of footnotes. There are a number out there to choose from, and many are quite good.
3. There are two questions to ask about each passage. Is there a command to obey? Is there a promise to claim by faith? If so, obey, and stand firm on the promises of God.

We do not need to make studying the Bible harder than it is. We really are without excuses today with the technology we have and all the resources that are out there. We can study from some of the most brilliant scholars with the click of a mouse. It won't just happen. You have to take the initiative to get started. It begins by becoming a regular reader of the Bible. Every day we should open it, read it, and let God speak to us. If we don't, we'll regret it. Just like a deer hunter hunting a piece of property every once in a while: he may sit in the right spot, but how much better could he be if he studied the land?

Chapter 8

Attitude

It was a cool fall evening in the Midwest. It was two days before the Illinois gun season, and I was hunting in Pike County, Illinois. My good friend was videoing me this particular evening. It was getting cooler, and the leaves were almost gone off the trees. The woods were noisy as you walked along. A squirrel sounded like a huge whitetail buck running your way. You've been there, haven't you?

I was about twenty feet in the air in my API tree stand. It was one of those nights where the weather and everything else seemed to be just right. We'd hunted this spot before. We'd seen several deer off this stand. I remember one little buck we called in about four times, with a doe bleat, on a previous hunt.

The sun was setting behind the ridge behind us. We were facing east. The wind was about fifteen miles an hour, blowing directly at us. We saw a buck about ninety to one hundred yards away down the hill, headed from north to south. He had his nose to the ground.

I grunted. He didn't hear me. I grunted louder. He still didn't hear me. I grunted again even louder, and finally he stopped. He looked in our direction, which was uphill for him. I couldn't tell what kind of a rack he had at this point. He started heading right up to us. I was blown away. He got within about thirty yards and started rubbing a tree with his antlers. The hair was standing up on the back of his neck. He was a big 6-pointer. He was about sixteen inches inside and had a G-2 on one side that was about ten inches. He was never going to be more than a 6-pointer.

When he quit raking that tree, he started walking to us. I drew my bow when he was about twenty yards away. I was full draw. He walked to about twelve yards and stopped. The angle I had was terrible, and it was a little brushy. He stood there for what seemed like an hour. It was only just under two minutes, but I was at full draw, mind you. He finally turned, and I let the arrow fly at twelve yards. The shot was dead on. The arrow hit right where I intended it to hit. That does not happen every time, but it's nice when it does. He ran down the hill, and I heard him crash!

I was overwhelmed with excitement, for several reasons. One, I had to hold draw on him for a long time. Two, it's not every day that a buck comes running to your grunt call. Three, he aggressively rubbed that tree at thirty yards. And four, he was visibly agitated due to the hair standing up on his back. He wanted to whip another deer. He didn't seem to be afraid of anything! I was glad to hear him crash. I had to sit down and think about all that had transpired before I could give my interview. I really had lost my composure. We finished the interview, and I climbed down. I followed the massive blood trail off the hill and found him piled up at the bottom of a good-sized hollow.

He was a ninety-one inch 6-pointer. I was as tickled with him as I could be. You won't see many any bigger than that. I did my final interview, and then it was time to make a plan on how we were going to get that rascal out of there. As I think about this buck, compared to other buck encounters I've had, I couldn't help but wonder what the difference was with this one. I've grunted at bigger bucks on numerous occasions and couldn't get them to give me a second look. What was the deal with this buck? I think one word sums it up: attitude! He had a bad attitude. He was like the guy who would fight at the drop of a hat and drop his own hat. He couldn't stand the thought of another buck being on his turf, and he came up to whip him.

In life, our attitude can help or hurt us. I remember hearing the statement, "Your attitude determines your altitude." I believe there's truth in this statement. You see, a bad attitude can cause you to sink, and a good one can cause you to rise even from the most difficult circumstances. When I think about difficulty—I mean a man who really had a rough go of things—I think of Job in the Old Testament. No one had it any rougher than Job. The book that bears his name opens with a bio statement that he was "blameless, upright, fearing God, and turning away from evil." He had seven sons and three daughters. He had seven thousand sheep, three thousand camels, five hundred oxen, and five hundred female donkeys. He was a man of great wealth and blessing. That is just what you would expect from a man who has feared and walked with God, right?

Then there is a conversation in heaven between the Lord and Satan, and Satan basically gets permission to do whatever, only he cannot touch Job. Well, it gets bad for Job about now. In a day, he loses every one of his children and all of his livestock! His whole family is gone. I cannot imagine the grief. He says in Job 1:21, "Naked I came from my mother's womb and naked I shall return there. The Lord gave and the Lord has taken away. Blessed be the name of the Lord." The Bible says that "through all of this, Job did not sin, nor did he blame God." Job had the right attitude toward God and life. This is amazing!

Just when you think it can't get any worse, here it comes. The next thing that is permitted will harm his own body. He is smitten with boils and uses a potsherd (a broken piece of ceramic material) to scrape himself. Job 2:9 states, "Then his wife said to him, 'Do you still hold fast your integrity? Curse God and die.'" She felt sorry for Job and wanted him to be put out of his misery.

Now surely his attitude will turn sour. Right? I mean, come on! A guy can only take so much. What does Job do? Here is his response: "You speak as one of the foolish women speaks. Shall we indeed accept good from God and not accept adversity?" The Bible states, "In all this Job did not sin with his lips." *Wow!* What an absolutely amazing attitude!

Then Job has three friends who show up who are really not friends at all. They think Job has some kind of unconfessed sin in his life. They challenge him and really don't encourage him at all. Job eventually has some questions for God, and the Lord answers him in such a way that humbles him. He acknowledges that God knows what's best. God restores his fortunes and then some. He doubles his livestock. Job lives to be 140 and sees up to four generations after him. There were no women fairer than Job's daughters. He was a blessed man. He waited patiently on God and kept a good attitude in the midst of suffering. How did he do this? He stayed focused, in the midst of these terrible circumstances, on God's character and goodness.

How can we do that? How can we have a good attitude in the midst of difficulty? I don't think there's an easy answer because of our enemies. Let's identify them. The Bible says we battle the world, the flesh, and the devil. The world here is referring to this world system we live in. It's a representation of the philosophies and the worldview mentality that exists. In many cases this is the Antichrist in its ideologies. For example, we who have a Christian worldview are in a small minority. A Christian worldview simply means we want to view everything as the Bible states it is and should be. We seek to obey what it teaches.

The world around us will say we need to give them a piece of our mind. A man I used to work with had a bad attitude, and it would breed discontentment among the other employees. One of his sayings he repeated often was, "I'll do what I want, or I'll do nothing at all." He also liked to say, "I was looking for a job when I found this one." He eventually was permanently laid off. Are you surprised?

We also battle the flesh. The flesh is the old nature inside us. As Christian leader Dr. Stephen Olford (1918–2004) used to say, "The old man is resident but should not be president. He is dormant and should not be dominate."

This is where temptation can get us. We see something that arouses the flesh, and instead of immediately cutting off the head of the snake, we linger, ponder, and maybe investigate—and all of a sudden, we're in sin. We battle against the flesh. When going through difficult circumstances, the flesh may say, "You don't need to take that. If God really loved you, He wouldn't allow this to happen.

You need to say something brash, get mad, do something, don't just take it."

Is that going to help matters? No it's not. You may be thinking, *Well, it sure will make me feel better.* No it won't. You'll make things worse in the process and regret not having the right attitude.

Ball games seem to be where we see some men battle the flesh, especially if it's your child who had a disagreeable call made against him or her. We can see the flesh resurrect in a hurry. Or maybe when you're working on something at the house that continually breaks down, the flesh tells you to get mad, throw something, get loud, cuss, and the like.

As one well-known preacher once said, "I have not said a bad word in a long time, but I was so mad today, if someone would have written one on a piece of paper, I would have signed my name to it." We have to learn to listen to the Spirit and not the flesh.

We also battle the devil or his demons. I, for one, am not naïve enough to think the devil himself is spending time tempting me. He is confined to space and time. God is everywhere all the time; the devil can only be in one place at a time. I would be thinking more highly of myself than I should if I thought the devil was trying to wage war against me personally. However, one of his demons could very well be trying to tempt and derail me. He could be getting me to think wrong things that will affect my attitude.

Has a bad attitude ever cost you something? Has it ever made your situation worse? It can do so in a hurry. I try to be realistic but positive and have faith that a situation can improve. My attitude is affected not by what happens in a day but by the way I think about what happens to me during the day. For example, let's just say your transmission goes out of your truck today. You have a choice to grumble and complain or to trust that God has a plan and a purpose for allowing this to happen. Maybe the guy at the shop who works on your car needs to see Jesus in you. If you respond in a mean or angry way to what is going on, he may think, *I thought this guy is a Christian? He sure seems uptight all the time.*

Or what if, as you're talking to him, you say, "I don't know why this has happened, but I'm trusting God has a plan and purpose for this." How does he leave your presence thinking differently about you? He may leave now, thinking, *Wow, these Christians sure do know peace. I don't have it. I wish I did.* This would have a huge effect on all people around us.

I am convinced that when we are commanded to "Do all things without grumbling and complaining," God has given us the means and power to obey. When we choose to have a bad attitude, it's simply that—our own choice. You can have a good attitude. I remember a movie scene from "The Ride" that had a man kicking a soda machine because it took his money. His comment was "Sometimes you just have to wail on it." A boy dying of cancer said to him, "Sometimes you just have to let it go."

That's it. Sometimes you just have to let it go. Remember the 6-pointer. He couldn't let it go, and it got him an arrow that passed through both lungs. There are consequences to having the wrong attitude.

How is your attitude? Are you overly negative and critical about everything? This will affect your wife and children in a negative manner. Your children will grow up emulating you. So fight for the right attitude!

Chapter 9

Achievements

My oldest son, Josiah, loves to hunt. He has a good eye for spotting game and can sit still like a rock. He has learned when to move and when not to. He is a lot of fun to hunt with, because he gets excited. I took him on several trips a year ago, but we didn't have any deer get within gun range. On a morning hunt we had hogs in at daylight, but I wouldn't let him shoot because we were waiting on a deer, but none came in that morning.

Do you know what he said to me? Sure you do. "Dad, you should have let me shoot the hog ..."

"Yes, son, I wish I could have, but I wanted you to shoot a deer. We can shoot hogs all year 'round."

We were down to the last day of the season for us. It goes out on Sunday here in Georgia, so I knew that Saturday would be the last day he could go. A good friend of ours, Mr. Larry Brantley, offered to let him go sit with him. He had been seeing some deer off his stand at another spot he hunted. I agreed to have Josiah there, at the gate, by four o'clock for the evening hunt.

Mr. Larry showed up right on time, and they headed to the stand. It was a double-ladder stand about a two hundred-yard walk from the gate. I was hoping he was going to get something on this particular night.

They climbed up to the two-man ladder stand. Josiah said the wind was in their faces.

Due to this fact, Mr. Larry said, "We won't have anything come in behind us."

Josiah agreed. They had been there about ninety minutes, and it was starting to get dark. Josiah thought he heard something them. Mr. Larry said he thought it was probably a raccoon or something. It was about 5:40 at this time.

Josiah, age 12 at the time, slowly turned and looked behind them, and there was a deer about twenty yards behind them. The buck was walking in their direction.

Josiah started to raise his gun, and the deer stopped and looked in their direction. Josiah froze! He sat still, and the buck eventually began to move again. He got to the side of them. He was about fifteen yards away, his broadside facing Josiah. He put the scope on him and touched off the .308. Boom!

Josiah saw a flash in the scope. Mr. Larry asked Josiah if he'd missed him.

Josiah said, "No, sir! I got him."

About that time, as the buck was running off, he began to wobble a little in the back end, and then they heard him crash in the brush! Josiah had shot his first buck! I was in the yard, and my phone rang. It was Mr. Larry. I knew by the timing of the call that he'd probably killed a deer.

Mr. Larry said, "You need to bring Josiah some oxygen. He's about to hyperventilate!" He briefly told me the story and said, "Come help us load him up."

I got my knives and coolers loaded in the truck and took off to where they were located. I was thanking and praising God!

When I showed up, they had dragged the buck from where he had crashed back to the stand. Josiah was grinning like an old mule eating briers. He was excited. It was what we believed to be a two-and-a-half-year-old 6-pointer. Nice body size and a decent rack. A really good rack for his first buck. I took some photos of him and the deer and got Mr. Larry in on one of them.

It was beginning to rain a little, just a light sprinkle. We loaded him into the back of my truck and headed back to camp. We took a few more pictures after we hung him up, and we went to work on him. He needed to skin him, quarter him up, and put him on ice. The men in the camp were excited for Josiah, and they were all congratulating him on his first buck. That is something he'll never forget.

A good deer hunter performs an autopsy to find out the cause of death. Josiah put a good shot on him no doubt. Where in the vitals did he hit him was the question. As I examined inside the cavity, I discovered his lungs were in near-perfect condition. As I looked further, I saw the top half of the deer's heart was gone. Perfect shot, and with that he gets a little deer blood on his face and a picture, right? Yep, that's exactly what we did! We also had to run by and show the Benton family his kill so they could celebrate with him.

Josiah's goal was to kill a deer and to kill a good buck. He'd hunted hard and put in the time. He stayed with it when he thought he would not get one and was rewarded. How important is it for us to set goals and prayerfully pursue them? Goal setting and a flexible pursuit is what I encourage people to do. Someone once said, "If you aim at nothing, you hit it every time." There's a lot of truth to that. Some people can be out of balance in this area. They can be too far to one side or the other. First they could have the mind-set that says, "It will be whatever it will be," which means why bother, why get involved, why set goals?

The other error in my opinion is to be too aggressive with goal setting and holding onto goals too long. This is what I mean: Let's say you set a few goals, and you realize the Lord wants you to move in a different direction. Some will mistakenly say, "Well, I set these goals and I must keep moving. What will people think?" That is why I said that I encourage goal setting but also have a flexible pursuit of those goals. The word flexible is the key.

Bottom line, I set goals to keep me moving in the right direction. However, if we discover in the process that we should be doing something else, that goal has to be modified. Do not foolishly keep moving in the wrong direction. Some people spend their whole lives climbing a ladder and halfway up realize it's against the wrong wall.

Instead of getting down and beginning to climb the right ladder, they keep moving in fear: fear of what others think, fear of failure, and fear of the unknown.

Proverbs 29: 25 states, "The fear of man brings a snare." A snare is used to catch an animal. That's what fear does to us. It traps us. God does not want us to live in fear but in faith to follow Him and His will. So if He is leading you to change and set new goals, go for it!

What about the fear of failure? I remember reading a book that Manley Beasley wrote on the subject of faith. He said he was in a conversation with God, and the Lord spoke to his heart about doing something, and it was a large task. He said, "I began to question God in fear. Lord, what if I fail?"

He said God spoke to his heart and said, "Who said you were a success?"

I am thankful that I had parents who pushed me to pursue work. My goal was to be a carpenter. I built tree houses when I was a kid. By the time I was seventeen I'd made a few pieces of furniture in my shop classes at school. I also tackled a couple of projects at home. Thankfully, Mom and Dad let me try this. They had confidence in my ability, more so than I did at times. I tore out a wall in the living room. I also enclosed a carport and built decks. Before long I was working for a construction company during the day and working on my own projects at night. When my workload increased to a size where I could sustain a living, I stepped out and created my own fulltime business. This had been a goal of mine since I was a young man. I loved this. I was my own boss, could set my own hours, and could hunt when I needed to with an outdoor company I was filming with at the time.

This was a stated goal. My goals now are to be the best husband, dad, son, and evangelist I can be. That means I have to study and learn in these fields. In these areas, there will be all kinds of specific goals that arise. Like finishing this book. I have set goals and timeframes for this, and some have had to be adjusted. However, the goal is to finish the book!

What do you believe God has created you to do? He has created all of us to do something. It's your job to figure that out, and when you do, take the time to sit down and set goals that will help you measure progress. Also, take the time to celebrate successes along the way as you reach your milestones.

I once had the privilege of talking with the late S. Truett Cathy, owner and founder of Chick-fil-A, in his office. I asked him what he would tell three young men about life and the pursuit of callings and careers. He said he was usually speaking to young MBAs and not ministers, so he would tell me what he currently told them. He said that we need to be passionate about what we do. He said to know what you want to do, and do it with all your might. Secondly, he said we need to get all the training in this field that is possible. And third, just do it!

Great advice. You eventually have to pull the trigger and do what you believe it is that you're created to do. Figure that out! Set goals! Find accountability! Get moving! You can do it!

Chapter 10

A Man Is Redeemed

I HAD JUST BEEN to the local Walmart to pick up a new youth model .243. I met my good friend Barry Benton to get it sighted in for my children to use while deer hunting. We chose the distance of seventy-five yards to sight in this weapon.

The kids were going to be able to go hunting the next day. It was the opening week of youth season. John had never shot a deer before. This gun was almost dead-on right out of the box. It was one of those scope-already-mounted and bore-sighted package deals. I was pleasantly surprised. We only had to shoot five rounds and we were ready.

Barry had been a born-again Christian for eight days at this point. I must back up and tell you a little bit about how we met and what he was like. Once you hear this story, you'll know that we serve a God who is large and in charge. I first met Barry at a storage building in Lyons, Georgia, on August 31, 2014. He was roped into helping us move some of our heavy items into our new home by his brother, Bill. While he didn't know me well at the time, Bill had volunteered himself and his two sons to help me move. When it came time, one of his boys was tied up with something else and couldn't make it. So Bill was thinking I needed some more help. He ran into Barry at the Dollar General across the road. He asked him to help us move a few items, and Barry agreed.

As we moved our belongings, I found out that Barry was an

outdoorsman, and a good one at that. He was impressed with my antlers, turkey beards, and so on. I saw him showing Bill as they were loading them. We connected that morning. He told Bill when he left that day, "I like that guy."

Bill began to tell me Barry's life story. He was rough. He'd been involved with drinking, drugs, and fighting his whole life. He was a man in the county that no one wanted to mess with. If he liked you, he would do anything for you. If you crossed him, he might just whip you and everyone who tried to get in the way. He was notorious for his ability to fight.

I used to hang out with people just like Barry, so I wasn't intimidated by him. He and I had a common interest in the outdoors. Bill would invite us to come over and watch football games on Saturdays at his house. Many of those Saturdays Barry would show up and eat. Usually he would fix a plate and go find a place by himself. Then he would leave to go hunt or place hog hunters who would pay to come in and hunt with him. When he would come fix his plate, I generally would fix mine and sit down and talk with him about hunting. I would ask questions and talk about things that interested him. We built a friendship. We started doing a little hunting together. When I had an opportunity to preach, he would show up and slip into the service.

He began attending a men's Bible study that I was leading. He got under such conviction that he quit coming. (This is what happened to me right before I became a Christian.) He asked his mom if she would get him a Bible. She was glad to do that! (His mom and family had been praying for him for years. Many of them thought they would get a phone call some time that someone had killed him due to the way he lived and people he associated with during those days.)

He began taking his Bible to the deer stand. I remember the excitement in his nephew, Bradley, when he told me he saw him with his Bible and was headed to the deer stand.

Barry was trying to change on his own. One afternoon he told me about a guy who came with his wife into a local Mexican restaurant in Lyons. He said the guy was drunk and was talking really ugly to his wife. Barry said, "Ronnie, I tried not to make eye contact with him because I knew if I did, we would be rolling around on the floor. I'm trying to change my ways." There was no doubt God was at work in Barry, convicting and drawing him to himself.

Not long after that, he was in an altercation with a guy who had a knife. The guy came after him, and Barry took the knife away from him and knocked him out. He was a salty character. He has been shot at and missed at close range. God definitely had a plan for Barry. We were talking and texting a lot. We were hunting together some.

One particular Sunday, our home church, Lyons First Baptist Church, was having a crusade at the local high school. We were inviting all the lost people we could. We arranged for Tony Nolan, an evangelist out of Woodstock, Georgia, to come speak that morning. I was scheduled to start a Sunday-through-Friday revival meeting in Reidsville about fifteen miles away, so my family and I went there. Bill told me he was going to do his best to get Barry to come.

I went to church, and we had a great service. When I got to my vehicle after lunch, I had a text from Bill. It read, "He got saved."

I texted, "Who?"

I did not want to be presumptuous. You see, I'd prayed and shed many tears for this man, and so did my family, along with many others. In fact, I have never wept over the condition of a man's soul like I did for him. He had become my most wanted for Christ. Thanks to my evangelism professor in college, I have a "Most Wanted for Christ" list. Barry was at the top!

In the process, Barry had become my friend. Bill sent me another text that read, "BARRY!"

I totally lost it as my wife showed me the text. I wept. My wife wept, and so did my children. These were tears of joy! It was unbelievable. He had been saved!

I spoke with him that afternoon. It was unreal how he had changed already. We talked or texted each other every day after that for a week. On Wednesday, we bow hunted together. On Thursday, he shot a very nice buck and sent me a photo while I was in the dentist chair. He came to the revival meeting Wednesday through Friday night where I was preaching. He brought his mom and dad Thursday and Friday night, and we all went to eat after at Dairy Queen. This was clearly not the same man from one week earlier.

He told his brother before he was converted, "I don't like to go to your church. They're always wanting to hug on me."

On Wednesday night when he left revival, he reached up and hugged my neck. On Saturday I took one of my boys and went to pick him up. He was letting me use one of his deer stands. He wanted to talk about some things. He told me how he had not cried since he was a little boy. That week he said he had "squalled like a baby" about four times.

He told me that when he shot that 124-inch buck with his bow, as he was walking toward it, he was overwhelmed and began to cry. He lifted his hands to the Lord and said, "God, all these years I thought I'd done all of this, but now I realize I would not have anything if it weren't for You." He said to me, "Is that normal?"

I chuckled with excitement and said, "Yes, and it's evidence that God has changed your heart."

We talked of numerous other things on that day that gave evidence that this man had truly been born again. He told me of his remorse for all he had done and the people he had hurt.

He said, "Ronnie, I've been a bad man, and I've hurt a lot of people." The pain on his face was evident. He was wondering how his friends would respond to his change.

When I saw him on Sunday morning, he was smiling from ear to ear. We made plans to get together to sight in the rifle I'd bought the children. It was the youth season and muzzle-loader season in the state of Georgia. After we got it sighted in, I drove him over and he gave me some deer / wild hog sausage he'd just made. I told him where we were going, and he said he and his dad were going on Tuesday morning as well. I had a text conversation with him that night. He wished us good luck for the next morning's hunt. He was excited for John. Barry loved kids, especially his grandson.

The next morning, John and I rose around five o'clock. We headed to Mr. Larry Brantley's house to follow him to hunt on the land leased by the Tanner Williams Foundation. This was a foundation started by some men when a local boy who loved to hunt was tragically killed in a car accident. They exist to take kids hunting, spend time with them, and point them to Jesus. I'm thankful for their work.

John and I went to what is called the School Bus Stand. It gets this name because about fifty yards away there's an old school bus. John and I got settled in, and as daylight began to break, the feeder went off at seven o'clock.

I texted Barry: "Feeder just went off. We're hopeful. Hoping to touch off the thunder stick!" We'd been texting back and forth off the deer stand for a couple of weeks.

He didn't respond, so I thought, *Well, he may have deer in front of him or already shot one.*

In a few minutes John, who was ten at the time, had a doe step out at 117 yards. She walked across the shooting lane too quickly for a shot. She then turned around and walked back. He had to wait for her to come out from behind a limb before he could shoot. I was coaching him. I told him as soon as she was in the clear, put it right behind her shoulder, about halfway up the body, and bust her.

She took two steps and stopped. As soon as she stopped, John squeezed the trigger, and she dropped in her tracks! This boy had just made a 117-yard shot! He was so pumped. He started shaking. We high-fived and celebrated. I was going to text Larry, Delana (my wife), and Barry. When I looked down at my phone, I saw I had four missed calls and three or four text messages from my wife. When that's the case, you know something's wrong.

I called her immediately, and she said I was to call Bill's wife, Rhonda, right away. Rhonda told me something bad had happened to Barry and that he was dead. Someone had murdered my friend in the middle of the night in his own home. Wow! I cannot describe to you how I felt at that moment. It was surreal. On one hand, I have my son by my side, who has just killed his first deer, and in my mind and heart I needed to celebrate that as best as I could.

I called Mr. Larry and told him what had happened. We quickly took pictures when he showed up with the golf cart, and then we loaded the doe up and headed back to camp. We decided to skin and dress her, leave her whole, put her in a big cooler with ice in the body cavity, and get to the Benton house ASAP. After years of dressing deer, it doesn't take long.

The Benton family was there, along with friends. It was a terribly difficult day.

There's not enough room to put here all that transpired that week. One of the discussions that kept coming up that week was that while this was tragic, how much more tragic would this have been if this had happened on Saturday, October 3—one day before he was saved? I am of the opinion that Barry's soul was not saved until the fourth. He was a Christian for just eight days.

There was as much evidence in his life that he was converted as any person could have. I was privileged to be one of the preachers at his funeral. There were others who were saved that day, and literally hundreds have been saved since that time because of the gospel and his story. My evangelist friend Tony and I tell it on a regular basis. It needs to be told. The matter of where one spends eternity is an urgent matter! I am thankful to the God of heaven that He pursued Barry and saved him before it was tragically too late. God snatched him from the fire that already was at his feet. We had no idea that he was on the verge of eternity. I thank God for His mercy and grace. I am also thankful for something good in the midst of something tragic.

I sure do miss my friend. One day I will go where he is. All because of what Jesus did for us. I needed Barry's life to intersect with mine to remind me of the importance of building relationships and sharing Jesus with people. Even with those who are the least likely to become followers.

What about you? Have you been saved? Are you living for Him? If not, and the Lord is dealing with you, would you come to Jesus now and receive Him with a repentant heart? If that's what you desire, just cry out to God and confess to Him that you're a sinner, and tell Him you're sorry for your sins and want to turn from sinning. Tell Him you believe Jesus was crucified, buried, and raised for you. Receive Him as your Lord and Savior.

If you do that, I want to know about it. I want to help you connect with a local church, follow the Lord in believer's baptism, and get you some material that will help you get started on your new journey.

Thanks for taking the time to read this book. I'm glad to be able to share a few experiences with you out of the rich treasure of life the Lord has given me. May the Lord bless you and give you peace.

Information Page for Ronnie Smith Ministries, Inc.

Ronnie not only writes but speaks on a regular basis. He speaks at wild-game suppers, men's conferences, and revivals. He would be available to come to speak to your church or men in your community. Contact him on his website. He also hosts a podcast "Rooted in the Word."

Visit him on Twitter: @ronniesmith70.

Visit him on Facebook: https://www.facebook.com/Ronnie-Smith-Ministries-Inc-113658598665709/?ref=br_rs.

Visit his website: www.ronniesmith.org.

Made in the USA
Las Vegas, NV
19 November 2025

34719832R00039